attraversiamo

Other Books by Monique Ferrell

<u>Poetry</u>

Unsteady—NYQ Books, 2011
Black Body Parts—Cross+Roads Press, 2002

attraversiamo

(let's cross over)

by Monique Ferrell

NYQ Books™

The New York Quarterly Foundation, Inc.
New York, New York

NYQ Books™ is an imprint of The New York Quarterly Foundation, Inc.

The New York Quarterly Foundation, Inc.
P. O. Box 2015
Old Chelsea Station
New York, NY 10113

www.nyq.org

First Edition

Set in New Baskerville

Layout by Raymond Hammond

Cover Art: "Attraversiamo", 8.5" x 8.5," digital art, © 2016 Raciel Guzman | racielguzman.squarespace.com

Library of Congress Control Number: 2016931044

ISBN: 978-1-63045-021-2

attraversiamo

Acknowledgments

the beast—*Token Entry: New York City Subway Poems*

airtight alibi—*Rabbit Ears: TV Poems*

minuendus: for the good men of new orleans—*American Poetry Review*

Contents

exodus

the badlands

For Lawrence, my Dad
It is as you will it—Hamsa.

attraversiamo

gilt…

a superficial brilliance or gloss

my childhood slid into the water today   just like that

did not   fold itself neatly packing up   to fit wisely into suitcases
heralding a desire to travel abroad   but instead   busted in on time
mortar   steel and brick   laughing at them along the way

we are foolish against the fluid   a mere lie in the face of the natural world
that can   in an instant   shame you into submission and it *is* shameful
standing powerless against a *fullthroated* gust of wind   that cannot be seen

but who   without mercy delivers your neighbors' roofs and corpses to your feet
your *business*   seen and unknown   to the public world

the petulant and running footsteps of your childhood   across a *shouldalwaysbethere*
boardwalk   are a mockery now   as you stand   out of doors and out of body

and it is stark

sitting standing staring   into the pitch as black night   the dark *alwaysmoving*

harness of water   tugging at your strength and courage   the fork-in-the-road moment
that asks you who you are   demanding that you bear and move bravely   toward the distant
but audible call of a human heart   crying   pleading to be rescued

by an even stronger human heart

what will you tell yourself in the morning sun

it was the wind rolling over rain   over the unhinged buildings   cinderblocks
amusement park rides   not the descending retreating *lettinggo* of someone

who used to be somebody else's child

what can you know   stepping out   into an unforgiving and defiant

cold morning   that adds insult to injury

what is there   but shame

because in truth   surviving isn't enough   you want *beforethis* back

your things back

your home on its foundation a parade of runners lined up   around the corner

untroubled and ready to burst forth

trains and buses lying about being *on or close to schedule*   you want this

want not to be the breaking news   or to have to explain to men in Washington suits
that you are worthy of their politics a vote cast   to make *this* nightmare a never was

for this is too much

it is too big   is why we rush into our parents' beds   as children

someone has to make the bad things go away   make *them* a never was

a ridiculous phantasm conjured up by id and ego

that has even freud laughing from his grave

instead   there is a broken knowing   that maybe

our parents should not have coddled us so   should have instead made us

remain in our beds

lights out

made to lay still

subject to the whims of our boogeymen and our courage

the beast

I am seeking a respite for my inner child here   but   I guess
we all are who are we kidding   the huddled masses yearning
to be free take up refuge on the underbelly of an underground
uptown/downtown anything   headed anywhere but where we
are going   and just *where* are we going anyway

set adrift like loose change from a pocket   uncomfortably close
and well-meaning waiting to be useful   to make sense

I am thinking these things   all while colliding into my neighbors'
memories and recollections   group therapy for two dollars and

fifty cents a swipe of a thinly veiled piece of plastic I read
these people as if they were my own   and I guess
they are like me   a too heady mixture of dread   inspiration

and the faintest scent of hope

a dangerous combination to mix with musk and metal   it's too easy
and combustible and yet they keep coming
telling lies and keeping secrets

excuse me ladies and gentlemen…may I have your attention please?

and it's what?   what now?

what socio-economical-ethnically-disenfranchised-politically-embattled
group needs me to stand in the gap for them today   I am my own
embattled group   a mess of ideas   longings

and you are interrupting the even exchange   a fast and *freeflowing*
body of ideas between me and my fellow citizens   can't you see
the gentleman seated next to me   has not bathed in days   not lately
not at all   in his recent understanding of time and space

the very nature of the world as he knows it tucked gently around him
protruding from   the holes of each trash bag   it is not safe
to be this disconnected   he from us   we from him   I breathe
inhale him deeply   with intent

I want to be responsible

across from me   an unforgiving woman is in her feelings   needing
waiting for a moment to lash out into the void of this confined space
looking at the midtown women about her   giant designer bags and
toohighheeled shoes   a *blackberryfull* of necessary
ideas   to pass the time   her contempt for them has no boundaries

she *assumes* at their joy

look at us   threadbare   lined up   seated   leaning
each of us searching through and around each other

we   long for magic

god help us   if we ever find it   catch a whiff of it   bouncing up off of
the stained station walls   or playing tag   with the florescent lights
there might just be a riot   and all of us just might

will   pry open these *pretendclosed* doors   while still in transit
waddle through   the dark sewage   baptizing ourselves along the way

take the stairs   maybe two   three at a time   up out into the promised
sunshine   and we all *might*   just keep walking   keep right on walking

until the earth changes its trajectory   spins us off into a new   a different
horizon   one where we are everyone's keeper   not a victim of their
silence   set to music in a confined space

but   until then   I sit silently   inserting myself into the lives of each
of my neighbors

wondering at their machinations   searching   yet again   for another dollar
that I barely have

and thank god it's catchy   we are all doing the same

the shoulder

the tender shoulder protrudes   maybe   this is defiance
is an arched effort   to say   *no*

I am not a still thing but am instead a beating and moving mass   of tissue
and cells   wishing to matter   of my own accord   just for this moment

or   maybe quite simply it was *this*

an accident of fate a response to the stifling heat   of your family's London car
so filled with   *you will nevers   here is your place   know the line*

but surely it wasn't a death knell

was not an entreat for blows leveled down   upon your brown flesh   by the familiar

as your stunned and *knowingbetter* siblings sat in silent awe   there had to have been
a collective memory   a once tender something   playing out in the background

a sharing of the familial and the familiar

once upon a time   you suckled at the breast of this   *breakingbonefist*   rode happily
upon the knee of your hangman   a giddy-up pleasure ride for a *good* good daughter
who would assuredly do good things   never disappoint

and now sweet sister   you are *this*

lying murky-minded relenting   for you will not fight back
listening instead   for their forgiveness   perhaps a reprieve
but hear instead   *just finish her* and you know now there is no coming back

just an end to this   *don'tunderstandlife*

and you are called past the light and onto an ocean of sounds
water slipping like laughter   between your toes

and god   is not ashamed of you   or by you
but is instead   the knowing breath of life

touching gently your bare shoulder

airtight alibi...

today   the world fell down or so the anchor woman said   her name was
heather or jane or roseanne   maybe   she hadn't put it just that way and my own
rhetoric is too cataclysmic   but   we are living in trying times

in trying times she said *it seems we are living several black men   did very bad things today*
or maybe she said *and here's today's top news stories* and I heard   prognosticated
the implications of color and crime   and hung my head   wondering what shade
of darkness   these deeds would bring upon   my shoulders

my shoulders   bear the stain of somebody else's crime the man who gunned his girlfriend
down   and tossed his baby out of the window   the serial rapist   stalking the dog-tired bodies
of graveyard shift working women   striding the stone's throw walk   from subway to home   and
on the anchorwoman went *knowing-it-all* at me   and then   the worst part of all

the worst part of all   are the expert artist sketches   that make you place a well-meaning
terrified hand   to your heart   until you come to your senses   reach for your phone
the villain   heather or jane or roseanne   tells you   is light skinned to medium brown
dark brown to dark skinned thin or heavyset   tall or short
maybe bearded or clean shaven   and this   is too close to the bone

to the bone skin deep either of these men could have been my brother my dear friend
or the man who shares my bed   I do not fear them   but I fear a world that does
and so I am calling *where are you? what are you wearing today? did you see that sketch?*
laughing at me they attempt to assuage my fears   but they know I'm right
know all too well   what they say   about black men in public spaces

public spaces are all we have left   the last bastion of   here is where you get to know me
that I am not a thief a batterer   a terrified fist into your seamless world   but am a man
with sisters a mother   women who turn to me for love and comfort   and because

someone loves me   I need to be seen   beyond the good intentioned craft   of an artist's pen
that imposes the bad guy's face   behind my good and safe eyes   there is no danger here

no danger here   today   as the sun sets   and all of my men are in their place
are through the day   without being ransacked   against a subway wall   cuffed or mistaken
before a viewer's prying eyes   masculinity   still intact   for the moment   the world still sees
them as I do nothing here to see   or that   heather jane or roseanne   can say

somebody's baby (no 1.)

momma's baby poppa's maybe   that's how the dozens dig used to go

I grew up on smells   saints and sounds   and the rhythms of amen jesus
played hallelujah happy   by the sunday baptist choir

if jesus   had tasted my grandmother's food   sat at her table   he would still be here
would have crawled down off of that cross

all full of vim and vigor   walked right on past his transgressors   laughing
taking his momma's hand firmly   he might have said   *aint no thang but a chicken wang*
winked at her   kissed her forehead and she'd know   beyond all doubt

that she had raised a man

a sticking around man   a *my word is my bond* man   but he wasn't raised on soul food
neither did he ever learn the dozens   his last words   tell us that

still looking up and around for his father   asking   *are you there? am I on my own? left behind?*

too sensitive for my family   I buckled easily   couldn't bear any insult   about my nappy hair
or big behind   my own comebacks   shaky and unsure   brought my
cruelseemingscoundrelofafamily   to their knees   with honest to god   gut slapping laughter

she said what? you were not built for this life girl. you sho' you black?

in the face   of so much certainty   I used my only power

I cried

hard tears   *howcouldyoudomelikethis?* tears   one day I'll show you   tears

it never stopped them for long though   there'd be another family function   or dinner
some reason or faux pas on my part   would set them at me again

maybe I used the term *faux pas* at the table   and what kind of kid from the hood does that
without wanting to be snapped on   called red bone   yella   siditty
not your mother's child   at all

my mother was the worst offender

knowingly between digs she'd give me that look

half wondering   if we were *really* cut from the same cloth

if I was indeed *ready* for this world

would maybe   end up like jesus   dying on a cross   for somebody else's sins

crying out for someone   who did not appear to be listening

while she   dumbfounded and powerless   stood in the crowd watching

minuendus

for the good men of new orleans

and so it is   that a man understands himself   knowing   that after the waters subside   it
will take the great weight   and magnitude of newly cleaned hands to harness these ruins

build   upon this kind of injury

and so he will dupe   his *allthetime* diligent conscience   into believing that mortar
and cinderblocks   are the tonic   for what ails you   *when*   what ails you is the bad ache
of bone   crushing down on bone   a mass exodus   into thunderdome
all the while   maintaining his composure with *excuse me* and *if you please*

some semblance of civility

when there is none to be found

and the women round about him   are looking for men to be   genteel benefactors

here   upon this grave midnight   certain to be the last   huddled together with women
who are not his own   while *his* own   he knows   have blown by   bloated and swollen
down bourbon street   the used to be world   becomes a dirty ocean   yielding nothing

ever the optimist   he says aloud   to no one in particular   but to anyone   who is listening
laissez les bon temps rouler imagining in his mannish heart   what he will build anew

astonishing   a now engaged world   with his arrogance   and stick-to-it-tive-ness
seeing   in his deceptive mind's eye   *a hand-of-god-shine*   where the mud
and decimation   once made a home

but the women around him   know better and are now looking upon a madman
who has lost much   to the unforgiving outside   he is but one person more   to look after

beyond themselves and the children   who are on their last diaper   bit of food

and very last bit of pretend

every woman here knows   these men will become   dangers to themselves now
malcontent   taking shape over *stillformingbone* discovering no promise   within
the receding waters   no hidden condition   about being free   from this

for a man knows what he knows   understands himself when a boy   that he is separate
from girls   he *is* a certainty   she a moving thing   subject to his whims

much like the water

and because he believes in *this* certainty   and it is validated along the way
he believes himself to be   a genteel benefactor

that he is courageous a winged hero   into the maelstrom of their nightmares

pushing back time and tide

a doer a fixer   not this   *allthetime standingstill* man   now false
in the face of the upending   of the whole   complete   and entire world

but   it is this *newday* daylight   the out into the very last dog-tired morning

the promise of rescue and removal   that finally costs one man his soul

having prayed for the sun and for dry earth to trod upon   it takes the raw
and privileged prying eyes of cameras

to tell a truth

that *all* is not well   with the women in his care   that there   is a new haunt in their
ancient eyes   one more debt that he can never repay   like being sold or running
away   chasing northern lights   that promise freedom

the dark depth of his generational silence

and now   this

he has become a man who cannot hold back water

keep it off of his roof   or out of his home   and after a today like today
not out of the eyes   of any woman he knows

but it is the overload   of fresh menstrual blood   heavy like more rain water   down so many
brown thighs staining ten-day-old clothes   that finally breaks his heart   into knowing

a man knows nothing really   and that his hands   slow and limited

could never really protect these women   now pushing the *playpretend* button

stoic faces before   a stunned world

they do not ask for this penance   this *sickwithsadness* man   now at their feet   stepping out
of his dishrags   using them to wipe   each woman clean
his own spittle   now ash   to bathe   their stained legs

they gather him up instead   this good man   who learned too much today

and carry him forward   as they always have   countless times   and generations before

attraversiamo

open and hungry   mouth agape   I stretch outward for a sign   it has been a while since
I've been delivered into something *soveryaboveitall* and   my soul is hungry

but who among us is not

for we are not children and because we are not children wing-ed and caped in our mother's
bed sheets and curtains we must try even harder to feed the hunger that lurches forward from
our breastbone in the midnight hour when the house is quiet and still

and the shadows on the walls and ceiling play fantastic

all our *still to comes* and lost ambitions working themselves out before us

god is comical

and is most clear when we are too dog-tired to do anything about it   but the truth
will not let us sleep   will not let us play peekaboo   with second chances

the moon   in all her fullness   accentuates the aggravating and necessary ache
while the stars bellow out a bluesy tune   ancient and known   to the willing listener

when are you going to get there they want to know and you know the answer
but you have been putting it off   out of fear maybe uncertainty   definitely

because your esteem has taken a beating lately made you believe a wrong worded lie

about yourself   and so what is there now

when you're as low as you can go and are beyond crying fits the jagged tears
and see yourself a warrior   against the sound splitting   now emptying void

what is there but to rise
from your bed and go there firmly into yourself
running into you along the way   embracing her every chance you get

emerge this new thing forgiving and uncompromised   and so very thankful for the ride

jink

1. To make a quick evasive turn.
2. Rambunctious play.

stunt

I want to cross over now   it should be a simple thing to do

wake up become self-aware   significant and *allknowing* every single good and halfway
decent futuristic sci-fi movie ensures the computers   will get there one day

know better than their masters

so when is it my turn

I have been waiting like a crooked coiled snake   in the corner of my life
waiting   to know better   to one day know it all

it was the promise made by grown folk
who ushered questioning children from the room   away
from their adult conversations

rhythms   sexual overtones   undertones   *decadeold* hurt feelings   harsh brutal
simple fatalistic language   that ruined families and friendships   started affairs   brought on
mental breakdowns   and ruined every family reunion and funeral of my childhood

you could never get close enough   to the core of anything   in my   *be seen and not heard*
you'll understand   when you're older world

adults never let children get close to the burning flame

forget the stove   it is life that is *catchfire*

and so   each child emerges all *seethrough* and witless   into a very real cutthroat world   believing that a
full set of tits   a hairy massive man chest   and monthly blood

are enough for   what ails you
but it isn't

from the center

the entire planet is on the verge of orgasm
I know this to be true
outside today I watched the great mystery unfold

butterfly couples engaged in a meaty give-and-take chase   that made me blush
wonder if my still-new-to-the morning eyes had all but interrupted something private

the personal

birds hovering in mid-air   and then holding firm in a *deathdrop* embrace
that could not be broken

is this what happens when we are not looking

the assurance that life will go on making itself manifest
doing its business without our authority   or intervention

for what could we possibly know
we only exist because they do

every seed planted acorn tucked away gentle worm harvested
becomes a fossilized moment in time
a deposit in the bank of life ensuring that all will move forward

even without us

and so it is   that their love making is necessary   is done in the daylight
they are not ashamed

why should they be   they understand the magnitude of their undertaking

it isn't always about pleasure   but is instead about staking one's claim
the imprinting of one's image onto the landscape of life

like now…

for I can bear their intensity no more
find myself both humbled and aroused by the audacity of nature

stumble across the threshold of the balcony of our Costa Rican hotel room
wander over to the still sleeping man
with whom I share this life   this time around

I will him even from the profound depths of sleep   that he is always aching for
bid him to notice me

come now we women have been at this for generations

long before stories about women and apples
wars and trojan horses

when first the heavy and heated sludge of life pushed forth from the waters
we had that knowing in our eyes

how best to coax touch   make tremble

opening his eyes he reaches up for me   and we
join the great echo that forms this life
calls to the next

and carries everything in between

carrie mae

we are our past in many ways   I see it in my face every day   suddenly
I have moved beyond first names   and everyone has become

sweetie precious darling honey lamb   and boo

and I didn't even see it coming   the transition into southern belle
Carrie's grandbaby   all *growedup*

in many ways   I still see myself a child   seated at the kitchen table

you   hard at work   in front of the stove   hunched over a sea of pots and pans
delivering some form of wisdom   to my insolent ears
fighting hard against hearing   if I had only known then

what a gift I had been given   to learn at the feet of the master
perhaps the hardgoing times   would have been easier   less severe   but as you often said
a hard head makes for a soft behind   and aint it the truth?

why didn't I get that sooner?

instead I took it to mean   that you were going to penalize me

for this   or for that

there is always some black girl infraction   that must be set right   before she grows up
to be a loose fool   strumpet   or some man's pleasure

ridiculous and full of folly

instead you meant   break the patterns   shy away from the things that you did the left turns that should have gone right

but I am an American girl and we like to do things the hard way
all hopped up on sex and the city and snow white
we grow up chasing the backs of men   are told they really love us

we just need to make them see

but with a wooden spoon in one hand and what had to be three sticks of gum
crackling between your teeth and tongue you laughed at me

mooning and full on weeping

over what you called *some nappy headed fool* humming you said

every shut eye aint sleep and every goodbye aint gone

and what did I do? ungrateful reckless beast of a child who had the audacity
to eat your food and live in your home   I rolled my eyes

and you loved me still

I was a silly mess worried about *he say she say*

but you told me to stand firm in front of the mean girls telling them

dig one ditch better dig two

I covered my ears in disbelief what is heartfelt *livedinbeenthroughitandsurvivedwisdom*

in the face of cruelty because your clothes are dirty are not as new and you are from the hood

but I wish that I had been braver if not for me certainly for you
on your knees on the cold floor of our bathroom every night asking god
to do what you could not

arrange what was beyond you

that's what all good women who know better do

make deals with an unseen god

hoping that he isn't really a man but is instead a woman who knows what it means

to have a daughter or granddaughter

set adrift in an unfriendly world that sees her as its prey

feminazi: gender studies 101

I learned something important today

I am a dirty word

an albatross about the quiet woman's neck
and my students taught me that

a simple lesson in gender studies   revealed to me   that feminists
are loud and angry man haters   that all women *hate* each other

and mothers must prepare their daughters   so that they can be attractive to men

and *these* were the words of my female students

I grow weary

looking out   into the sea of well-meaning faces I cross myself
and I am not even catholic anymore

with puzzled eyes   the girls accept without question
that they are doomed to hate themselves   and their sisters

they cannot for the life of them explain what it means to become a woman

and because they can't   they allow themselves to be defined

and so

they are defined   generation to generation   across race and class here

the boys in the room   exchange knowing looks
brazenly backslap each other

confident that they will always rule the world

and I'm not so sure they won't

deja vous, again

I saw twenty-five yesterday   and she wasn't fooling anyone

standing *funnyfooted* in her *toohighheeled* shoes   with the red bottoms
multicolored from head to toe   because someone told her it was in style

was the fashion was couture

her hair   not her own   her *own* not her own   I wanted to fight her

and I do not mean in my mind either

I wanted to lay her to waste   as she stood there

uncomfortably shifting   from foot to foot   her toes
possibly bleeding in her *wellmeaningshoes*

checking again her watch   against her patience   she smoothed and comforted
the announcing itself *waytoobigbag* someone told her she needed   caught sight of
herself in storefront glass and seemed if only momentarily   to realize

that this   was all   too much

that she was in fact not ready   for the world

and *this* is when I loved her as any woman over thirty-five would   and should

stop and feel compassion for the *old self* she sees   in the *way too lost for this life*
younger women she walks this world with   how busy are we

to not grab these young tender women by the shoulders shake them loose
from the unseen   predicament of their lives

it doesn't get better we should say it gets good and hard   unbearably frightening

in an *all lights out* armageddon kind of way

run home immediately   cast your yesterday doll babies   your happily ever after stories
with the ratted pages   your beauty mags and your *selfhelp* guru books

into the fire   and dance around the embers   as if your life depends upon it

because it does

no good no true comfort can or will come to you   unless you are willing

to do this

to live   as if you are already everything you need

submitted for your approval...

an ode to rod serling and the twilight zone

dark suit   cigarette in hand   the man in the shadows beckons
this black and white dream   live and in color   portends a dubious outcome for us all

and we are spiders to his fly   victims of our own curiosity   we know   what *this* is
the deep slide into the black seeded   scalding heart of humanity

in the night   in the midnight hour   so pitch that your own hand
is invisible before you   he calls   telling us   that *we* are wrong

across the galaxies   in other dimensions   face to face in the full-length mirror
in the depths of the deep woods alongside of the sparse country road

we are wrong

and so imagine this if you will he suggests   a hint of smugness
dipping across *thealwaysinplace* grin   that we are just like *them*
that *they*   have always been us   or that the phantasms are indeed real

are not the voices of our conscience
but the real life monsters made true under our very own beds

with ash stained fingertips   he points the way to redemption
but   we are always too late and the man   who knows too much   for his own good

turns on his heels   leading us toward   another jagged day

marsha, marsha, marsha...

those steps go where? I asked my grandmother

rerun tv is a bona fide trip in the ghetto   ever clarifying making crystal clear
who you are   where you live   and what you do not have

the image of mike carol *alicethemaid*   six kids and a dog   traipsing up and down
a sure and true   set of stairs leading off to more rooms   more parts of the house
and places to sleep   was too much for me   what could I know of such things

while sharing   a room   and a bed   with other bodies

for one year solid   I pretended my apartment was *anotliketheother*   part of our
housing development   a transition from room to room

had me *deepstriding* a set of pretend steps of my very own
much to the chagrin   of our downstairs neighbors

and to the dismay of my belabored grandmother   who pondered the stretches
of my sanity   and the burden of living in poverty

but what was she to do?   you cannot compete with a happy mom   a dad who stays
and siblings   who do not seem to know   just how good they have it

so the brady's became the goal   *this is what you work for* she would say
a man who will not leave   a home that isn't bursting at the seams   with hungry mouths
someone   to do your cooking   when your feet   are tired

I do not know what I would have done   without the rerun scenes of my youth
wonder woman was beautiful   superman could fly

and the hulk wasn't scared of anybody

but   the bradys had a home
arealhome free of bullets and theories   speculations about future prospects
while wading   through piss and feces on the way to school

every kid from the hood knows   they'll never fly

that the bed sheets tied about our necks   are just that

and so we quickly put away these fantasies

but we understand the way things *should* be

that we should not live under the gun

or behind one

that we deserve a set of stairs   doors that close
the sound of a house at peace

the rise and fall of sleep throughout that same house

and someone nearby   to care

run...

just a few words for doctor who and his delightful companions

what else could you do   but want him   stepping out of the darkness   into your life
a self-proclaimed madman in a blue box   that is so much bigger   on the inside

bigger than your own humdrum   made from minutia life

powerless before him   you take his newly formed hand and enter into his
newlyformedeverythingofalife   no time for subtleties or formal introductions

it's *an are you in* kind of day

will you die kind of moment

you stand on tippy toes   and stare firmly into those   *catchfire* eyes
step off into a life   that was always meant to be your very own   off into a trot
that breaks free into a sprint   unfolding into a maddening *fullthrottle* run
his hot   two hearted alien breath   on the nape of your neck *singsonging* in your ear

run   run for your life...

and it is your life   that you've been running for   running toward
away from the people who think they know you best   away from clicking keyboards
bad almost marriages   a world you *know* must surely spin   in the other direction

a corner not turned

what you have needed   all your life   is *this* someone to teach you   to master your fate
captain your soul   that you were right as a child   you are *indeed* special

a savior
and saver of worlds   a prophet   a giant   god...

and he will never tell you otherwise   a madman with bloodstained hands
and no home   needs a conscience

with two hearts   he will feel much   and you must stave off the wilderness of remembrance
and so it is   that the introduction   must always be this way

a cannon burst of footsteps   but you are wearing your good shoes today   it is easy to keep up

to move forward   never once looking back   holding the hand of   the last timelord
in the universe   *everybadthing* there is   giving chase

everything you've always wanted   before you

exodus

awethu (to us)

for Madiba and Malala

I.

I know what revolution feels like   we *step* to it skillfully
even if at first we are cowards trembling hard against a dark heart
roaring up like a lion   in the bush

without fear   there is no need for courage

no need for the brutal damaging gut   that journeys out   toward the undefined
thing in the distance   it is a revelation defined within the womb
when we are blind full of faith   still tethered between our mothers
and the land of our gods

and while some sip from a golden chalice   or walk in safety   sleep effortlessly
in their beds   have bells knell out their inherited birth right   across the continents

for us there is a darker road   one that must be beaten out
forged by our search for grace and mercy

born into ignorance and ghettos   bullets are the wind chimes that *singsong* our existence

we learn   we are entitled to little   and mostly nothing
our first words read like sedition and treason   against an unfeeling world
built to keep us in our place

and so rebellion becomes the mantra

into the troubled lands we are placed becoming the fine razor
used by fate to mete out justice   or have it carved into our collective bone

so what are twenty-seven years away from a family   babies sitting at the hipbones
of their mother a woman whose knowing eyes say more than her mouth can

that she will carry on   become a warrior in your absence   while you stand a martyr for the cause

what are twenty seven years in a jail cell   the blue sky outside mocking you
pretending at the heaven beyond it   you know separate is not equal
that children are dying in the streets   women are using sticks bricks and stones

against soldiers politics and the rules

and they beat back the villainy of circumstance and lines drawn in the sand
while their men toil against the fates   that have fooled them   and have so foolishly
and with contempt   knit together an unbearable lie

made your black skin a blemish

you will not forsake this life   nor hang your tender neck from your prison sheets
you know your name Tatu Rolihlahla   the future and reconciliation are in your hands

II.

if you can… wait   count…   keep your dignity

how best to maintain your dignity   in a world that insists it knows you   better
than you know yourself   believes that you have somehow negated and surrendered
your modesty   because you use your voice like a hammer

and because you use your voice   like a hammer   you are shot down like a beast in a field
like a dangerous thing   because you are dangerous
know that words have meaning   are like light and life behind a young girl's eyes

in a dark and desolate world   that wants her bent   defined   lied to   small

a wrecking ball in the lives of other girls

and you do not know how many more times   they will strike at the life you have been given
once   twice more   beyond the sixteen years you have already lived   you do not know

nor do you care

understanding only this   that you must speak   that in this moment the faith and fate
of every girl in the world   lies in your tender hands

wrapped in Benazir's shawl   you said to the shadows   who crave your silence and your soul

nothing changed in my life except this   fear weakness and hopelessness died

III.

and for you today   I count the seasons of my life   like rings on a tree   hoping that my own roots are
strong enough   to withstand the troubling tides   once upon the horizon

now at our doors and our feet

the hawk in search of my soul   the hissing at my ankles in the tall grass that surrounds me

I do not know   how to be anything but black
never wanted   to be something more than woman

I fear a world that is not ready for me   for us   everywhere
out there   looking for the way in

somebody's baby (no. 2)

for hadiya and trayvon

when they are born to us   we do not believe that we will outlive them

no parent ever does

instead   we are concerned about the lessons   we must teach
how best to keep up with the ever changing fads   so that
they are never   on the outside of the little worlds   they so treasure

and we stack ourselves like brick soldiers between them   and

the cruel world that is no place for poets   dreamers   the tenderhearted

and   so it seems   our children

we designate safe spaces for them to trip and tread   give these places
easy sounding names like home and school that make the falsehood believable
and they acquiesce   feel safe   beyond our reach   our careful touch

but just today we blinked

found him walking about the house spreading out like a man   confident in himself
and about all the days laid out before him   stepping out into the world
a long and heavy mist on his shoulders   we let him go

into the waiting and hungry arms of the very thing we warned him against

when he was younger we looked under the bed   behind the curtains

inside of the closets

pushing aside hanging clothes   and old toys that looked like heady illusions
to sleeping child   trying to be a man in his big boy bed

and so we ruffled his hair left the nightlight on

told him we were just down the hall   or right next door

and he believed us

closed his eyes and was comforted

but we did not check beyond the front door   down the block around the corner
that fateful day   because we blinked   and just like that   he was gone

and so was she

and it was raining that day too

she did as was she was told   what she had learned from us
to take shelter   keep safe   when the world is out of sorts

we helped her choose her outfit that morning
even though she stopped needing help   a long time ago

made her breakfast   wished her good luck on her exams

and thank god   we stopped to say I love you

because the days had become so busy
and there was work to be done
and we hadn't slept   money was tight

because of these things

it makes it hard to remember sometimes   that you have to stop

count the kindness

remark for a moment   on the years you've had her   held her

and now to know   that you sent her into the world   into the arms of the hangman
who gunned your baby down

a baby himself   unknown to her   looking to cut down someone else's baby

and she was in the way

taking shelter   as you had taught her

and was she thinking of this wondering where we were
unable to tell the bullets from the *hardhitting* raindrops

I don't want to pray anymore

the world is no place for poets   dreamers   the tenderhearted

and   so it seems   our children

they *are* ours   *all* of them

we ride the blackness for them   endure the night so they won't have to

and it seems a shame to live in a world   that can so easily cast them aside

ici, dans le métro…

I'm not surprised anymore by what I see   this sacred space is the laundry mat of the world
here the colors blend and bleed we mix   not heeding the outside voices   or label warnings

we watch each other spin   and it is dangerous is
a rich world of feeling   and so we pay for the intrusion

the man across from me winks   it is deep   filled with meaning
this will not be followed by a come-on
he wants me to know that he is a man   announcing himself against the strength of this steel box

hurdling through the tunnels   at what feels like the speed of light
he wants me to see him see myself as he sees me
for this is what men do
the doors open   and we exit each other's lives

a glutton for punishment   I ride on

to the right of me   the Sirens sit   dressed in their summer fairest   each of them weeping

and it is elegant

they entered   smelling of fifth avenue pressed and pampered   pedicured manicured
each crying into well-meaning handkerchiefs   that are not up to the task of their grief

this is how all women should cry

their sobs are silent everything about them pleading *why*   to a god that does not answer
that cannot hear them below ground   at the center of the earth where all things are amplified

I curse the thing that inspired their hurt   looming there on the other side of
the once again *closing doors* that I must *stand clear of*

must be a man… no a child

men make women scream   make them dangerous to themselves
women lose their voices over their children
I am safe from this kind of madness   yet to be blessed with this kind of tragedy

wanting to enter into their pain so desperately   I begin searching my bag   offering Kleenex
and lozenges   no one should mourn alone

but like everything and everybody else   they too are carried away
beyond the always closing doors

in times like these   music offers no solace   no separation from the masses
that are now   body to body   much too close for the over there rage
of someone   that is bleeding through my now useless earbuds

he is begging   angry   slamming his body against the poles
against those unable to move quickly

I can't imagine what it means to *want* like this
but we are tired   have been told this story before   we are no longer believers

are not up to the task of being our brother's keepers today
are now made impregnable   petrified by the soot and skepticism

we do not mean to be this way   each waiting for our stop our chance to leave this place
for the doors to fling open

and to be carried away

the silence

for mason

nobody knows how to do this   how could they

this disaster of a reckoning   with the flesh   the *bitterbreakingdown* of the mind

is a testament to your learning   a new thing

hard against it you push   each time   a gentle nudge   reminding him

I am your son   this   is your wife

as if stringing him across the *winterfog* of his own thoughts while tethered to *your* words
your memories   are enough to bring him through this

back to you   the way it was

learning a father   with   massive hands

who teaches you that a man a real   and knowing thing   loves through his work

with his hands   shift after shift   at a plant   or in the Chicago sewers   on his back
under cars   grease and soot   the compost of life   edged firmly   into the creases
of his body   hard harsh backbreaking sledgehammer work

barely enough coat   to cover his own bones

lunch pail   crooked in his arms like a baby   against the frigid *almostday stillnight* light
he looks   confidently over his shoulder   knowing that all is
well with his house   the babies are warm   there is morning breakfast for his gentle
wife's hands   all because   he is a man   against time

a *one day we'll look back at this   and wonder what happened to men like this*   kind of a man

and so you learn to love   this way too   with a heart   bigger than your hands

bigger than your checkbook   but that has never stopped you
for you have learned   from the best

a giant

goliath himself has taught you how to make something   out of nothing

that there is enough for everybody   and so your home is always open
your ear always pressed against the phone   across neighborhoods and state lines

and everyone   knows

that you are the great rock   upon which they all stand

and because you are the great rock   have done more with less   have been a man
against time   *a one day we'll wonder what happened to men like this*

kind of a man

you thought   life owed you something   owed you at least the privilege
of watching your teacher leave this world   as a man

not this

and so it is *hardgoing* for the both of you

for you know somewhere   he is in there

somehow   he is telling you *this is so shameful son   so hard to the bone*

but what   can you do

nothing   but what men have done across time   when no one is looking

shed   your armor   and be tender

take hold of this man   who tiptoed into your room   as you lay sleeping
told by your mother that some unknown draught had   *fevereduptheirbaby*

and   like a man he touched your head   hot to his fingers   bent low
kissed you gently   told you   that he would do more
so that his son   would not suffer   would never be caught off guard again

you know how to do this   to love between the shadows   to make clean what
illness has laid bare   he is you now   you are his father   a tried and true

everything of a man

the nightwalkers: for the children of uganda

"…and either I'm nobody, or I'm a nation"—Derek Walcott

we   a great orgy of bodies suspended in fitful sleep   await either god or death
I am wondering now   if they are not one and the same

what is anything to me now   but this thick wave of black flesh   skin indistinguishable
from the earth   upon which we sleep and trod endlessly   all good things

are broken now

being one whose future depends upon the vertebrae bones   of the child who walks
before me   every night   before the sun sets   upon this *ashfilled* nation

I understand only   the bowed head of vigorous concentration

one foot   in front of the other   this is the way

while your mind tries not to dither upon   the uninterrupted massacre   of the past

but you cannot help but to remember

the *stillwarm* rifle butt   at the base of your skull   as you are ordered to wrench apart
the world as you know it   the greedy soldier's *lusting pinklips*   eyeing your mother
and *tooyoung* sister   while still another pisses upon your father's remains

his fists   still balled into hammers   as if even then   he could at once rise

from death

to defend what was his
and now you   *a less than man*   tear filled and fouling your own clothes

are ordered to use your tender hands   to lay to waste   what remains

do as you are told   or else

and you know what *or else* means   your mother and sister are beautiful   and you
will not see them soiled   *yes do it*   mother says   *do it and live*

the plea from her mouth   replacing the terror in her eyes

they are holding hands when you deliver the first of many death blows   and you continue
until they are unrecognizable   until there is nothing left of their bodies

to be desecrated   by you   or any stranger

until   you are sure that your hands are bleeding   that you have devastated   and
pulled every usable muscle   in your body

and you are willing   to meet hell   willingly

and so it is months later   running like a wild dog   into the unforgiving bush
fleeing from my sleeping captors   I returned to them   filled with envy and shame

resenting   the peace of their deaths

loathing   that I had not done more   to stop them

and I said these things to them   *cradledcupping* their bones   laying them next
to one another   as if posing them for a family photo   in which I would take no part

shedding everything that gave me a name   watching the embers   burn into flames flame into a shocking emotion   that almost took me into its bosom

I remembered then   an *always gentle* lady's   last request   that her miserable son live

and that is when they found me

this restless band of children   but a stone's throw from my own age
shooed away by *still living* parents   people who are left to give a damn

refugees   hugging the dark walls of this unbelievable world

in which we all now play a part

asylum   sanctuary   safe hold   safe house

these now   are the bread   breath   and bone of life

is what we sing about in made up songs   with the *almostuseless* words of our language

and   as we sing   walking   endlessly walking

I count their heads   their shoulders   the distinctive patterns of their feet

but   especially   their bones   the bones of each back before me

I will know them fully and completely   if and when   they go missing   into the night

will then ache for each   as I did my own
while I am alone with my dismal thoughts   amidst a sea   of *stilldreaming* dark bodies

fingertips touching   legs almost kissing   sighs filled with sleep

hundreds of near babies   taking the place of those who are unable to love us

for just this moment

all   patiently   awaiting the dawn of a new   and terrified day

giant

for every woman

what are we now   standing on the precipice   a jolt of lightning   flashing before our eyes
and we   are no longer daddy's little girl   or the next generation of our mother

if ever we were those things at all

perhaps we were always women

fully formed and ignited   fathom deep and full of meaning

the grand conscience of humanity

I can live with that   standing   running full throttle   into the detailed mystery of life

but what I won't be   is inconsequential

limited   redundant   a statistic   the other end of a brutal and *badmeaning* fist

instead I choose goddess

breakingbig across life   as did every woman before me
knee deep in cotton fields   heads held aloft   looking past the rigidness
of indentured servitude   with a necessary patience

on sick, death, and dying beds   *childbearing beds*   the fierce brick of prison walls
stadiums   podiums   arenas   classrooms and offices

in this generation   or that one   or from the bottom of the dark mud
that snatched us forth   and named us life
every woman calls to the next   knows the other by name   believes
there is work to be done   that nothing is gained by our silence

our living small   or terrified

our bargain with god is greatness   an embracing endorsement
of all our sisters everywhere everyday   today

this   is prayer

without it we are clouded   the last to know   *everwaiting* in line

without tickets to our own performance

every woman calls to the other   and knows her name   the one we hear

but ignore

in the cracked spaces of our heart
that even we   don't visit anymore

it is here   at our sisters' knees that we learn our true meaning

that we are not meant to stand still

for no giant ever has

the badlands

hey, little girl...

for my goddaughter, Nena

hey, little girl   what do you believe about yourself today

what untruth *wrongwordedthing* defines the magnitude of you
as you stare into mirrors and shiny surfaces   laid flat at your feet

what *wrongworded* thing do you believe

they have made you into an empty catch phrase   full of nonsense and ridiculous
so unlike you gestures   made you believe   made you *almost certain*

in your deep down places   that you are altogether wrong

that you do not know your own mind   the relevance or significance of your
wondrous thoughts cascading like unimaginable   great equations

across the electric sky

almost daily attempt to bully you

into believing   that your beauty must be boxed in   constructed   into a
lukewarm   generic version   of the *pretty-face-of-the-hour*

when instead you defy tradition   and old renditions

you cannot be fathomed

your face does not always bend serenely toward the light
sometimes it enjoys a challenge
your voice   will not always stand in someone else's shadow
it craves a stage   and observation

your hands thick   strong and giving   know the magnitude   of good and great works
and your body *well* that is yet another   good and great work

misunderstood and marketed   it too must be heard

taken for what it is

a multi-layered

voluminous

full and heated

cacophony

of everything good   everything worthy

generous and accepting   from head to toe

and do you hear me little girl   little *somedaywoman*

there is only the universe   and   *this* voice that speaks   to you
traveling across the mighty distance
with every fiber of its knowing   and being

and you little one   the carefully placed and meaningful thought

are there in between

tutti...

no don't do that   keep focused I say to myself

one hundred and eight beads to count the world   this is what dawn is for
but it is *hardgoing* today   and the mighty *om*   isn't enough

I am told that buddha   sat like this   under the bodhi tree   waiting

to bump into himself   into god   life   the meaning

his luck was better than mine

for I do not like what I am seeing   behind closed and meditative eyes
but   I am told to press on   this is what revelation requires   a willingness

so I submit   attempt to censor the dark thoughts   in order to make   this daily trip
around my hands   one hundred beads now   into and against the silence

but it is *hardgoing* this morning

each bead is defiant

becomes an omen a distrustful little pearl that shines a light   on those
with whom   I share this planet   *submit* I say   one person changes many things

chases evil

evil   with its dirty little smirk   something behind its back   an extra ace up its sleeve
or behind an ear   while on its way out of the door   or window

knowing that this isn't goodbye   merely so long   *aberightback* hat trick until you yourself are burdened and waiting   wildly attempting to block out the madness

like a woman being gang raped   on a bus in india

a man thrown from a train platform to his death   while someone took a picture

a movie theatre   burning with gunfire and discord   the cool winter night as backdrop

and now this

the unspeakable   that I count down to eighty-eight beads

a hardness forming   over my own soul

until each bead becomes   the face of a child   cut down and slaughtered

on a school day   crayons and backpacks strewn about   used to block

heated metal and rage

why do churches stand   any temple synagogue or shrine exist

what good is a holy place or these tiny stringed circles in my hands

aren't we quite broken beyond repair or the fingertip of god

he she or they   it seems   are no longer listening   and *we* did that

I wouldn't listen either

tuning in to us is asking for heartbreak

we've no further left to fall

have already jumped the shark   mastered genocide   are fluent in suppression
excel at self-righteousness and condemnation

it is *hardgoing* for us all

but I continue to count these beads because I know that god *isn't* listening

but *wants* to

and imagines that at least one of us is clinging   to a mala or rosary is lying prostrate
singing or chanting on behalf of everyone

and if one can do that   on behalf of everyone   *in spite* of everyone

then it is worth these   between yesterday and today mornings

no one in the house awake   but me

and these dismal thoughts   the pearls crisscrossing through my fingers

and maybe just maybe there too is the lingering breadth of god

heavy boots...

we ought not be so casual with our history it is dangerous

finds us fumbling for our bearings if not our tender sensibilities

it always catches me off guard and that is when it hurts

like when you are sitting in first class called by your title   handed a glass of wine
asked for your preferences and are not feared

one is comforted as you are flown over an ocean

forgetting that you hover above the graveyard of your people

thrown over castoff self-drowned

leaning back in a *biggerthanmybody* cushioned seat I fold into ancestral memory
overhear the white men in business suits behind me   laughing about slavery

honestly one of them said   *my youngest son was just fascinated to learn*
that we used to actually own black people

upon further listening I would learn that said son was excited to deliver the news
to his black best friend   the very next day   I couldn't imagine what that would be like

a child at play building blocks coloring books everything limitless before me having
something like that crash into my understanding   of myself

we used to own you sell you beat you rape you steal you lie to and about you
sometimes toss you when done with you haphazardly into the very waters
my father flew over yesterday want to play?

I should have said something... anything

like I learned to do   with older male coworkers   who called me sweetie and hon'
or men who expected a response   because they have leered at me

called me boo or baby   or whatever the nom de jour

but it is sometimes easier to push gender over color   race strikes at the tender
makes us defiant and defensive   and alone in our judgments

and so we are careful   almost too careful   and are all the time hurting feelings
pulling at the tattered wares   of what we think we know   about how everyone should feel

but what to tell a man   merely telling his son   about how it used to be
that his tone   should be more grave   that he should cross himself   while passing

over these now sacred seas

that we've all paid too heavy a price   to so easily laugh about a thing like that

as if it were something *weird* we had to pass through   before we could get to happy

but I said none of this

merely stood   pretending to search for something in the overhead compartment
pulling at the tether   holding my dreadlocks atop my head   I let them fall to my shoulders

let my gaze pass between myself   these men

sons and a daughter of a hateful past

taking my seat I said to myself   in what could have been no more than a whisper

I am here   they were here

all of us   now looking out and over into the water   we moved on in silence

papers please...

when a tree is felled   it never expects to be desecrated

for it would beat back the bearer   of the ax with limb and root
if it understood better the human condition

that we could carve out a womb   made to tread water

carelessly swell the belly with life and limb   smooth out the hull of that same ship
until its body   cool and flat with edges crisp like razors could hold the weight

of a still yet another people

blood soaked   by the foreign etchings of   *my word is my bond promises*
that would never   be honored   in any corner   of the world

and in every corner of the world   spread themselves thick and thin   wrecking their way
like a plague through forests and formations primeval that existed before man   could blink

growing ever wiser is the true abomination

learning to understand   that homesteads colonies or manhattan condos and duplex apartments mean
little   that paper was the true master   diviner of faith and fate   could buy and sell

cripple an emperor or his economy

and now this

it issues a demand of show me

show me your papers please

show me mister president   *leader* of the first world indeed

interloper socialist fascist another *hitlerinthemaking* kenyan   bend over
cough   show us your teeth   crack open   your chest

down to your heart   we know it is black

is not fair   is not of us   our ilk   or strain

and   where are you going   little ladies

made privileged by a vote   it is a reckoning   we will soon revisit

your head is too high   set aloft with big ideas   bare instead   your breasts   strip down
accommodate us   pay no mind to your being   more than half of the world

most abused   most neglected

we prefer you in your *redbottomed* shoes   your delicious wigs and weaves

brought to you by the violation of your middle eastern and asian sisters

show us your documents   the reason why you are entitled to more

or dominion over your own bodies

like thunder   we are coming down   creeping up upon the immigrant

each and every one of their kind

never mind that we are all immigrants   brought here   thrown here   sentenced here

you just keep minding the fields   the crops and vinyards   busing the tables   fighting the wars
sitting in the classrooms   waiting   to be more

part of   the alleged grand design

just keep going   about your business   and while you are going   where you are going

do stop and show us your documents   your raison d'etre

we are keeping tabs

files on all of you   find your individual folders are lacking   in the concrete   the substantive
we know you better   than you know yourselves   understand paper

its nature   the culpability fullness of its measure

and know truly the sin was never in the woman   the bearer of the fruit

nor in the tree   neither branch nor root

but in the eater the bender of time and tide   who could so shift

everything and everyone in the world

like men...

the crowd of elders   gathered   they were *others*   only a moment before
headed off   to do this   or that

and it made me think   perhaps   some long ago   *a rift in time ago*

on a dark continent   *others*   just like them   gathered too
swelling with pride   as the youngsters   assembled   each waiting patiently
for the allowed moment   to assert their right   to be men

in the dust   of our could have been *usedtobehome*   feet stood firm arms flailed
as the boys   performed acrobatic feats   into a tug of war

earthcoloredbodies   displayed   their strength   if bested   they shook hands   embraced
living   to fight another day   but that   was some *other* time   and this was altogether
something else   an anomaly

here   the elders gathered in amazement   and

it's so difficult to be amazed anymore

like the little boy   in the Disney movie   asked by the frustrated *usedtobe*   superhero
just what he had   the unmitigated gall   to be waiting around for

I don't know... he replied   as only a child can   disheartened   and in desperate need   of an
adult   to make good on a   promise   *something incredible...*

incredible   was what we were witnessing   two young black males

circling one another   fists balled before them   not a gun in sight   stunned
the elders   bumped shoulders   eyes wide   mouths agape   an awesome silence
leaping forth   from their bellies   until they began   to chant

like men   fight like men   like men   fight like men…

and so they did   lunging   swinging   *halfknowing*   what to do

because   it had been so long

and then   the connect   a shake of the head   a heated grin   affirming that
each could take a punch   a hit   that wasn't delivered by a *brokendownlife*

until they collapsed in upon each other   both running toward   the embarrassment
of realizing   that you are not the baddest *blackmotherfucker* on the planet
or toward the reward of knowing   that you are bigger than a bullet

what could it all mean   how would this moment change   everything   forever

we would never find out   the sirens arrived   took them   and the potential   away
and we   like   the little boy   in the cartoon   were disheartened

I've heard   that the mighty blue whales   almost destroy themselves

during mating seasons

pick each other apart   *allbut*   blinding and debilitating   their foe

until the female makes her choice

and then   just   as suddenly   when the fighting is done   they embrace
an expression of tenderness   that borders on erotica

with great care   from stem to stern they touch   caressing the ancient and new hurts

84

as if to say   *I didn't mean to cut that deep*

they   do not hurry for you cannot rush forgiveness

it requires intention

and the pleading utterances   that shudder forth   from these massive bodies

until all is let go

I wish it were like this for *our* men

but we are not interested in their boo boos and scrapped knees

let alone their tears

we are instead   transformed by the magnitude of their ferocity

and vengeance

titillated by tyranny and bullying

and it's such a sad thing
for us all

haboob...

god has not forgotten us   she is being held at gunpoint
folding and unfolding her hands   counting universes
she thinks only of mercy   while on the other side of the gun
the hammer is cocked   bullet loaded in the chamber

and her thoughts are not for herself instead they are for the shaking hand
of the bearer of bullet for she knows how all stories end
and that between the hostage and the taker
she alone is the *baddest* of the two

I have had this dream often and never see how it ends

but I have a feeling

and for this I would be swept away   in order to forget

for I know the meaning of darkness that the City of Lights lays bleeding
in her very own streets   now covered with a sheet of flowers that despite
their best intentions are no match for what was done there

we must stop lying to children

for somewhere everywhere   corner to corner across the globe
there is someone   all make and manner of someones   willing to die
in the name of their god   while pleading the case and cause of god

and she folds and unfolds her careful hands   meditating on universes
and thinks of how we lie to children

and for this I would be swept away   and be less careless

paying more attention to the mayor who says *we cannot tell someone*
that they cannot live on the street and I would ask him what he meant
by that but he's always on the road has little time for us

and I have become too cautious and careful terrified by the sight of nakedness
soot and rags the collapse of many minds as they surrender
to whatever gets them through the day

the old man in the train station hits his crack pipe every time he sees me *every time*
he wants me to know

careful to keep his distance he points at me and mutters only
and always at me what he alone can understand

but I get it I blame me too

and for this I would be carried away

blighted

my body black body black female body does not matter today
is hunted and falls down while running skipping or walking away
corner to corner and across the globe

and now I see too clearly
the words of my prophetic and clever grandmother
who too moves behind careful hands while counting universes
days are numbered do end and she a jesus kind of woman
believes that *someone must be martyred for the world*

but if we must be in the business of martyrdom   could it **not** be done
by the people for whom this task was not designed
not those on their way to work   sitting in classrooms   holding hands
making love   laughing   fingertips on fruit and food stuffs   while at marketplaces
those just simply about their day

martyrs do not only die   sometimes   they choose suffering endure much
in order to speak   must speak   seek words   what else are the artists of the world for
but to suffer   by way of words on paper   paint on canvas
brilliant cacophonic notes played through the willing instrument

but we *must* have things our way

hopped up on lattés and the bloody kardashians   the real housewives... of
insert name city or state

jealously we guard actual feelings about things   that soon pass away and
are replaced by something else   that too will soon pass away   we do not believe
in steady things or each other   rather   we touch through data and profiles
because we are terrified of contact
and so our hands disappear   and soon too do our voices

the only dad I know   died last year   it doesn't matter how it was too soon
and it almost carried me away

on what I knew   but denied   was his death bed   we talked of this and that
because he knew too   it didn't matter that he was too young wasn't finished
had more to say   his story was ending   so he told me this: *write*

three days later he was gone

and it all blew down about me   covering me   knocking me about   until I realized
that sometimes you have to stop fighting the tidal wave   in whatever manner it comes
sometimes you just turn   and ride defiantly into it
using all manner of words to describe the grand terribleness of it all
as it strikes at your senses

the awesome mixed up terribleness of the world   the loss of someone you love

and this is when the dreams began

about me and god in the alley   I know now it's me and god   alone and together

the thinkers tell us we are everyone in our dreams

and so I am less terrified these days   when I dream them

but each time I go back there to the tiny space that feels less like a threat
it seems like neither of us are on our knees
but are keenly aware of the goings-on   outside the walls around us

and I'm pretty sure that neither of us is issuing demands or ultimatums
and the gun is looking more and more like a pen
and it is she   that is doing the pointing

and I'm not sure   because we're not supposed to entirely hear the voice of god
you know
because we're ridiculous limited human beings

but I believe she's whispering and the carefully
tempered and offered word

feels an awful lot like   *write*

Monique Ferrell

is a poet and fiction writer. She is the author of three books of poetry: *Attraversiamo,* (2016), *Unsteady* (2011), and *Black Body Parts* (2002). Her writing has appeared in *American Poetry Review, North American Review, Antioch Review, Cimarron Review,* and *New York Quarterly,* among other creative writing journals, as well as the anthologies *Token Entry, Out of the Rough, The Place Where We Dwell,* and *Rabbit Ears: TV Poems.*

Beyond her creative writing pursuits, Ferrell is co-founder of *2 Bridges Review,* co-editor of the feminist criticism text *Looking for the Enemy: The Eternal Internal Gender Wars of Our Sisters,* and author of a myriad of scholarly publications on writing, race, gender equality, and pop culture issues including the forthcoming book *The Seduction Deduction: Erotica, Intellect, and God-like Transformation in Arthur Conan Doyle's Sherlock Holmes and Dr. Watson.* Currently, she is a Professor of English and teaches Literature, Gender & Sexuality Studies, and Composition in New York City. She is also working on her first novel, *Tuck,* which focuses on the impact of mental illness and depression in African American families.

About the Cover Artist

Raciel Guzman is a native New Yorker. He comes from a rich Mexican cultural background and is a self-taught illustrator. He is a freelance artist whose work consists of creative illustrations and graphic design. Most recently, he worked as a Graphic Designer for the Faculty Commons at New York City College of Technology, City University of New York (CUNY).